On the Go! jokes for kids

Also by Whee Winn

Lots of Jokes for Kids
Lots of Knock-Knock Jokes for Kids
The Super, Epic, Mega Joke Book for Kids
Lots of Christmas Jokes for Kids
Lots of Tongue Twisters for Kids
Lots of Jokes and Riddles Box Set

ZONDERKIDZ

On the Go! Jokes for Kids
Copyright © 2019 by Zondervan

Requests for information should be addressed to:
Zonderkidz, 3900 *Sparks Dr. SE, Grand Rapids, Michigan* 49546

Softcover ISBN 978-0-310-76950-7
Ebook ISBN 978-0-310-76951-4

Interior design: Denise Froehlich

Printed in the United States of America

---

19 20 21 22 23 /LSC/ 10 9 8 7 6 5 4 3 2 1

Introduction

Looking for some fun? Want to be silly? Giggle a little? Belly laugh? Then you've come to the right place. We have done all the work for you—we put together the perfect collection of jokes, riddles, tongue twisters, knock-knock jokes, and one-liners about things that go on the road, in the air, on the water, and all things travel. And this collection is even more special because every joke in here is good for everyone . . . from your best friends to your parents to your teachers. *On the Go! Jokes for Kids* is just the place to find good old clean and corny jokes to entertain your friends and family for hours.

Our mouths were filled with laughter,
our tongues with songs of joy.

PSALM 126:2

Table of Contents

1

On the Road: Cars, Trucks, and Bikes

What part of a car is the laziest?
The wheels—they are always tired.

What kind of car does an egg drive?
A Yolkswagon.

What did the tornado say to the car?
Want to go for a spin?

How do fleas travel from place to place?
They itch-hike.

What would you call a country where everyone who lives there has a pink car?
A pink car-nation.

What would you call a country where everyone lives in their cars?
An in-car-nation.

Knock, knock.
Who's there?
Carl.
Carl who?
Carl get you there faster than a bike.

What do you say to a frog who needs a ride?
Hop in!

What goes through towns and up hills but never moves?

A road.

Knock, knock.
Who's there?
Colin.
Colin who?
Colin all cars. Colin all cars.

———————

Johnny was racing around the garden on his new bicycle.

He called out to his mother to watch his tricks. "Look, Mom! No hands! Look, Mom! No feet! Aaah! Look, Mom! No teeth!"

———————

Where do Volkswagons go when they get old?
The old Volks home.

Knock, knock.
Who's there?
Cargo.
Cargo who?
Car go "beep, beep!"

**What do you get when a
dinosaur crashes its car?**
Tyrannosaurus-wrecks.

What did the dinosaur say after the crash?
I'm so saurus.

**What did one stoplight say to
the second stoplight?**
Don't look—I'm changing!

What do you call a laughing motorcycle?
A Yamahahaha.

What did the muffler say to the car owner?
"Boy, am I exhausted!"

When is a car like a frog?
When it's being toad.

Knock, knock.
Who's there?
Wanda.
Wanda who?
Wanda where I put my car keys.

What has one horn and gives milk?
A milk truck.

What do you call a group of cars?
A clutch.

What snakes are found on cars?
Windshield vipers.

What does a cyclist ride in the winter?
An icicle.

"I will have to report you, sir," said the traffic officer to the speeding driver. "You were doing 85 miles an hour."

"Nonsense, officer," declared the driver. "I have only been in the car for ten minutes."

What kind of car drives over water?

Any kind of car, if it's on a bridge.

What kind of driver doesn't need a license?
A screwdriver.

**Why did the police officer
pull over the U-Haul?**
He wanted to bust a move.

What kind of car does a Jedi drive?
A Toy-Yoda.

A dad is washing the car with his son.
After a moment, the son asks his father, "Do
you think we could use a sponge instead?"

Apparently I snore so loudly
it scares everyone in the car I'm driving.

When is a car not a car?
When it turns into a driveway.

**What do you get when you put
a car and a pet together?**
A carpet.

What does a bicycle call its dad?
Pop-cycle.

What did the jack say to the car?
Can I give you a lift?

**Why did the man put
his car in the oven?**
He wanted a hot rod.

Knock, knock.
Who's there?
Isabel.
Isabel who?
Isabel necessary for riding a bicycle?

Where are cars most likely to get flat tires?
At forks in the road.

How do you stop a dog from barking in the back seat of a car?
Put him in the front seat.

A woman was driving her car without her headlights on, and the moon was not out. A man was crossing the street in front of her. How did she see him?
It was daytime.

Why is driving with one headlight not a good idea?
It isn't very bright.

Why did the little boy take his bike to bed with him?
He didn't want to sleepwalk anymore.

Knock, knock!
Who's there?
Falafel.
Falafel who?
Falafel my bike and cut my knee.

What happens when a frog parks in a no-parking space?
It gets toad away.

Knock, knock!
Who's there?
Iona.
Iona who?
Iona new car!

A truck driver was driving along the freeway.

A sign comes up that reads "Low Bridge Ahead." Before he knows it, the bridge is right ahead of him and he gets stuck under it. Cars are backed up for miles.

Finally, a police car comes. The officer gets out of his car and walks around to the truck driver, puts his hands on his hips, and says, "Got stuck, huh?"

The truck driver says, "No, I was delivering this bridge and ran out of gas."

Why can't a bicycle stand up by itself?
Because it's two tired.

What's worse than raining buckets?
Hailing taxis.

_____

I was walking down the street today when a tow truck pulled up alongside me. The driver said, "Excuse me, I'm looking for the accident site involving a van carrying a load of cutlery."

"No problem," I said. "Go straight down this road for one mile, then take the first left, and when you get to the fork in the road you're there."

_____

What has ten letters and starts with gas?
An automobile.

Knock, knock.
Who's there?
Parker.
Parker who?
Parker car in the garage.

Where do cars go swimming?
The carpool.

What happens if an ax falls on your car?
You have an accident.

What do you get if you cross a bike and a flower?
Bicycle petals.

A man's car stalled on a country road one morning. When the man got out to fix it, a cow came along and stopped beside him. "Your trouble is probably in the carburetor," said the cow.

Startled, the man jumped back and ran down the road until he met a farmer. The amazed man told the farmer his story.

"Was it a large red cow with a brown spot over the right eye?" asked the farmer.

"Yes, yes," the man replied.

"Oh! I wouldn't listen to Bessie," said the farmer. "She doesn't know a thing about cars."

What do you call a man with a car on his head?
Jack.

What do you call a pastor on a motorbike?
Rev.

What kind of cars do cooks drive?
Chef-rolets.

What kind of car does a dog hate?
CorVET.

Why can't motorcycles hold themselves up?
Because they are two-tired.

What's the hardest part of learning to ride a bike?
The pavement.

Knock, knock.
Who's there?
Philip.
Philip who?
Philip the gas tank—it's almost empty.

What do you call a pig who got a ticket for dangerous driving?
A road hog.

What do you get when you cross a Mustang and an elephant?
A convertible with a big trunk.

Where do dogs park their cars?
In the barking lot.

A rich snail goes into a car dealership looking for a new car.

The salesman shows him their fastest cars, and the snail settles on one. He pays in cash, but he has one request—he wants a big S, for "snail," painted on each side of the car.

The salesman can't help but ask why the snail wants something so peculiar.

"Because," said the snail, "when I'm driving fast down the highway, I want people to point at my car and say, 'Look at that S car go!'"

How do you put a car back together in Scotland?
With Scotch tape.

What kind of shoes do cars like?
VANS.

A San Francisco driver following taillights in a dense fog crashed into the car when it stopped suddenly. "Why didn't you let me know you were going to stop?" he yelled into the mist.

"Why should I?" came a voice out of the fog. "I'm in my own garage!"

2

On the Go:
Boats, Planes,
and Trains

Why did the airplane get sent to his room?
Bad altitude.

What do you call it when a giraffe swallows a toy jet?
A "plane in the neck."

Why were the railroad tracks angry?
Because people were always crossing them.

Which train car has antlers?
The camoose.

What happens when you wear a watch on a plane?
Time flies.

What did the doctor say to the man who got sick at the airport?
It's a terminal illness.

Why couldn't the steam engine sit down?
It had a tender behind.

What is as big as a steam locomotive but weighs nothing?
Its shadow.

What detergent do sailors use?
Tide.

Why do oars fall in love?
Because they're row-mantic.

What does a houseboat become when it grows up?
A township.

What's the worst vegetable to bring on a boat?

A leek.

**Why did the librarian get
kicked off the plane?**
Because it was overbooked.

Knock, knock.
Who's there?
Ivan.
Ivan who?
Ivan working on the railroad.

What do you call a sneezing train?
Ah-choo choo train.

Knock, knock.
Who's there?
Levin.
Levin who?
Levin on a jet plane.

What happened when a red ship crashed into a blue ship?
The crew was marooned.

How do trains hear?
Through their engine-ears.

Why did the ship's admiral decide against buying a new hat?
He was afraid of capsizing.

Why was the train engine humming?
It didn't know the words.

Knock, knock.
Who's there?
Wenceslas.
Wenceslas who?
Wenceslas train home?

What happened to the man who took the train home?

He had to give it back.

**When does a rabbit go exactly
as fast as a train?**
When it is on the train.

Where are the Great Plains located?
At great airports.

**When you go scuba diving, why do
you fall backwards out of the boat?**
Because if you fell forward, you would still be
in the boat.

Knock, knock.
Who's there?
Mandy.
Mandy who?
Mandy lifeboats, the ship is sinking.

What is the difference between a locomotive engineer and a teacher?
One minds the train, the other trains the mind.

How do locomotives know where they are going?
Lots of training.

What do you call a flying police officer?
A helicopper.

Why couldn't the sailors play cards?
Because the captain was standing on the deck.

Why don't elephants like to ride on trains?
They hate leaving their trunks in the baggage car.

Knock, knock.
Who's there?
Sid.
Sid who?
Sid down—you're rocking the boat.

An electric train is traveling south.
Which way does the smoke go?
Electric trains don't make smoke.

How do you make a boat feel better?
Give it some vitamin sea.

The train was about to pull out of the station.

Swinging a large bag, a young man managed to reach the train, throw his bag in, and climb aboard, gasping for air.

Seeing him, an older man said, "Young man, you should be in better shape! At your age, I could catch the train by a gnat's whisker and still be fresh. Look at you, panting away."

The young man took a deep breath and said, "Sir, I missed this train at the last station."

Where do you take a sick boat? To the dock.

Where do zombies like to go sailing?
The Dead Sea.

How do you find a missing train?
Follow the tracks.

**What kind of stories should
you tell on a boat?**
Ferry tales.

**Where do ghosts
like to go sailing?**
Lake Eerie.

What do you call a train full of bubblegum?
A chew-chew train.

**What's as big as an airplane
but weighs nothing?**
Its shadow.

How do rabbits like to travel?
They take a hare-plane.

**What lies at the bottom of the
ocean and twitches?**
A nervous wreck.

What gift do you give a train conductor?
Platform shoes.

How do trains drink?
They chug.

When you need me, you throw me away. When you are done with me, you bring me back. What am I?
An anchor.

What do you get when you cross a helicopter with a skunk?
A smelly-copter.

What is the difference between a school teacher and a steam locomotive?
The school teacher tells you to spit out your gum, while the locomotive says, "Choo choo choo!"

3

On the Job: Buses, Tractors, Police, and More

SCHOOL BUS

What has four wheels and flies?
A garbage truck.

Why didn't anyone take the school bus to school?
It wouldn't fit through the door.

A man trying to get on an overcrowded bus is pushed off by the people inside. "There's no room," they say. "It's full up!"

"But you must let me on!" shouted the man.

"Why? What's so special about you?" they asked.

The man replied, "I'm the driver!"

Who makes a living by driving their customers away?
A taxi driver.

What would you get if you crossed King Kong with a skunk?
I don't know, but it could always get a seat on a bus!

I just met a nice steamroller operator.
He was such a flatterer.

What bus crossed the ocean?
Columbus.

Knock, knock.
Who's there?
Mister.
Mister who?
Mister last bus home . . .

ER doctor: What brought you here today?

Patient: What do you think? An ambulance!

Did you hear about the magic tractor?
It turned into a field.

How do eels get around the seabed?
They take the octo-bus.

What game do monsters play on the bus?
Squash.

**A man was a limo driver for 25 years
and never had a single customer.**
All that time, and nothing to chauffeur it.

**Did you say that you fell over fifty
feet but didn't hurt yourself?**
Yes—I was trying to get to the back of the bus.

**Want to hear a
construction joke?**
I'm still working on it.

A police officer pulls over a car that's creeping along at 22 miles per hour on the highway.

There are four old ladies inside. The three passengers are all wide-eyed and white as ghosts.

The driver says to the officer, "Officer, I was going the speed limit! What seems to be the problem?"

"Ma'am," the officer replies, "you weren't speeding, but driving so much slower than the speed limit can also be dangerous to other drivers."

"Slower than the speed limit? No sir, I was doing the speed limit—exactly 22 miles an hour!" the old woman explains.

Chuckling, the officer explains to her that 22 was not the speed limit, but the highway number. Embarrassed, the woman thanks him for pointing out her error.

Before he lets them go, the officer asks, "Is everyone in this car okay? Your passengers seem awfully shaken."

"Oh," the driver replies, "they'll be all right in a minute. We just got off Highway 148."

Bus passenger: I'd like a ticket to New York, please.

Ticket seller: Would you like to go by Buffalo?

Bus passenger: Of course not. I'm in the line for the bus, aren't I?

What's worse than raining cats and dogs?
Hailing taxis.

Does this bus stop by the river?

If it doesn't, there'll be a very big splash.

What would you have if your car's motor was on fire?
A fire engine.

What's the difference between a cake and a bus?
I don't know.
Well, I'm glad I didn't send you to pick up my birthday cake!

What is the difference between a bus driver and a cold?
One knows the stops, the other stops the nose.

Passenger: Will this bus take me to New York?

Driver: Which part?

Passenger: All of me, of course!

A fire started on some grassland near a farm in Indiana.

The fire department from the nearby town was called to put the fire out. The fire proved to be more than the small-town fire department could handle, so someone suggested that a rural volunteer fire department be called. Though there was doubt that they would be of any assistance, the call was made.

The volunteer fire department arrived in an old fire truck. They drove straight toward the fire and stopped in the middle of the flames. The volunteer firemen jumped off the truck and frantically started spraying water in all directions. Soon they had put out the center of the fire, breaking the blaze into two easily controllable parts.

The farmer was so impressed with the volunteer fire department's work, and so grateful that his farm had been spared, that he presented the volunteer fire department with a check for $1,000. A local news reporter asked the volunteer fire captain what the department planned to do with the funds.

"That should be obvious," he responded. "The first thing we're going to do is get the brakes fixed on that old fire truck!"

How did the farmer find his lost cow?
He tractor down.

Why did the farmer roll over his fields with a steamroller?
He wanted mashed potatoes.

Why is a traffic officer the strongest man in the world?
Because he can stop a ten-ton truck with one hand.

Which end of the bus is best to exit from?
It doesn't matter—both ends stop.

**Why are there always two
EMTs in an ambulance?**
Because they are a pair o'medics.

Why did the bat miss the bus?
Because he hung around for too long.

**What vehicle is the same front-
to-back and back-to-front?**
A racecar.

———————

Person 1: "Quick! Call me an ambulance!"

Person 2: "You're an ambulance!"

———————

While the pope was visiting, he told the limo driver he had the sudden urge to drive.

The driver would never dream of questioning the pope's authority, so the pope sat at the wheel while his driver got in the back.

They were traveling down the road, going between 70 and 80 mph, when a police officer happened to see them. As he pulled them over, he called into headquarters reporting a speeding limo with a VIP inside.

The chief asked, "Who is in the limo, the mayor?"

The police officer told him, "No, someone more important than the mayor."

Then the chief asked, "Is it the governor?"

The officer answered, "No, someone more important than the governor."

The chief finally asked, "Is it the president?"

The officer answered, "No, someone even more important than the president."

This made the chief very angry, and he bellowed, "Now, who is more important than the president?!"

The officer calmly whispered, "I'll put it to you this way, Chief. I don't know who this guy is, but he has the pope as his chauffeur."

Have you seen the bus website?
It's just the ticket!

Did you hear about the wooden tractor?
It had wooden wheels, a wooden engine, a wooden transmission, and wooden work.

What did the bus driver say to the frog?
Hop on!

What starts with an M, ends with a K, and has a hundred letters in it?

A mail truck.

What do you call a sleeping bull?
A bull-dozer.

Two fish are in a tank. One of them asks the other, "Do you know how to drive this thing?"

4

Out and About Around the United States

Why does Mississippi see so well?
It has four Is.

What did Delaware?
I don't know—Al-aska.

Really, what did Delaware?
A New Jersey.

What rock group has four guys who don't sing?
Mount Rushmore.

What city has lots of sand?
Sand Francisco.

Knock, knock!
Who's there?
Iowa.
Iowa who?
Iowa you a dollar.

What did Tennessee?
The same thing that Arkansas.

Where does the president send his dirty laundry?

Wash-ington, D.C.

What is a dog's favorite state to travel to?
New Yorkie.

**Which state is round on the ends
and high in the middle?**
Ohio.

The library—it has
the most stories.

**What is the tallest
building in New
York City?**

Knock, knock.
Who's there?
Ida.
Ida who?
It's Idaho, not Ida-who!

What is the smartest state?
Alabama—it has four As and one B.

Why is it easy to get into Florida?
Because there are so many keys.

What happens when the fog lifts in southern California?
UCLA.

Which state produces the most cheese?
Swiss-consin.

What do you call someone from Detroit who talks a lot?
A Motor City mouth.

Who did Mississippi get married to?
Mr. Sippi.

Knock, knock.
Who's there?
Missouri.
Missouri who?
Missouri loves company.

What state do pencils come from?
Pennsylvania.

What is the capital of Alaska?
Come on, Juneau this one!

What is the cleanest state?
Washing-ton.

In what US state can you find tiny drinks?

Mini-soda.

Knock, knock.
Who's there?
Tennessee.
Tennessee who?
Tennessee you tonight?

Where does Dracula go when he visits New York City?
The Vampire State Building.

Where is the best place to dance in California?

San Fran-disco.

A man went on vacation to Texas for the first time.

He went to his hotel's restaurant and ordered a glass of something to drink. The waitress brought out a pitcher, and the man's jaw dropped.

"Pardon me," he said. "I ordered a glass, not a whole pitcher."

The waitress simply said, "Sir, this is Texas. Everything is bigger."

When the waitress brought out his meal, the man said, "Excuse me, I ordered a steak, not the whole cow!"

Again the waitress said, "This is Texas. Everything's bigger."

After he ate, the man went to find the bathroom, but he went through the wrong door and fell into the hotel swimming pool.

"Help! Help!" he screamed. "Don't flush!"

What is the capital of Washington?
The W.

What is the happiest state in the US?
Merry-land.

Where do Mississippi fish keep their money?
Mississippi River banks.

Knock, knock.
Who's there?
Utah.
Utah who?
U talking to me?

What is in the center of America?
The letter "R."

Where do eggs go on vacation?
New Yolk City.

What is the smallest state in the USA?
Mini-sota.

What is the loudest state in America?
Illi-noise.

What do you get from an Alaskan cow?

Ice cream.

5

On the Go
Around the
World

What is the fastest country in the world?
Rush-a.

What is purple and 5,000 miles long?
The Grape Wall of China.

Why don't you ever see penguins in Great Britain?
Because they're afraid of Wales.

What cow doesn't give milk?
Moscow.

What is the coldest country in the world?
Chile.

Knock, knock.
Who's there?
Norway.
Norway who?
Norway will I leave until you open this door.

Where do sharks go for vacation?
Finland.

What sort of dessert roams wild in Canada?
Moose.

**What do you call little rivers
that flow into the Nile?**
Juveniles.

Knock, knock.
Who's there?
Jamaica.
Jamaica who?
Jamaica me crazy with all these jokes!

What city always cheats on exams?
Peking.

**What is the biggest
rope in the world?**
Europe.

- -

Where do germs like to go on vacation?
Germany.

Knock, knock.
Who's there?
Kenya.
Kenya who?
Kenya open the door?

Where do sheep go on vacation?
To the Baa-hamas.

What is in the middle of Paris?
The letter "R."

Why is England the wettest country?
Because the queen has reigned there for years.

Knock, knock.
Who's there?
Wooden shoe.
Wooden shoe who?
Wooden shoe love to travel to the Netherlands?

Why was the man afraid to travel to Finland?
He was afraid he would disappear into Finn air.

Where do hamsters like to go on vacation?
Hamsterdam.

What happens when you throw a blue hat into the Red Sea?
It gets wet.

Knock, knock.
Who's there?
Oman.
Oman who?
Oman these jokes are bad!

Where do ants like to go on vacation?
France.

Teacher: What can you tell me about the Dead Sea?

Student: Dead? I didn't even know it was sick!

What vacation destination is yellow and likes to sing? The Canary Islands.

Knock, knock.
Who's there?
Francis.
Francis who?
France is a country in Europe.

Who is a penguin's favorite relative?
Aunt Arctica.

What is the biggest pan in the world?
Japan.

6

Away from Home on Vacation: Camping and Fishing

Why can't you run through a campsite?
You can only "ran" because it's past tents.

**Can a frog jump higher than
an average tent?**
Of course! An average tent can't jump.

What do you call a girl who catches fish?
Annette.

**Why are people who go camping
on April 1st so tired?**
Because they just finished a 31-day March.

Why are fish no good at basketball?
They're afraid to get too close to the net.

A boy and his father are sitting around a campfire eating a meal.

The boy asks his father, "Dad, are bugs good to eat?"

"That's disgusting. Don't talk about things like that over dinner," the dad replies.

After dinner the father asks, "Now, son, what did you want to ask me?"

"Oh, nothing," the boy says. "There was a bug in your soup, but now it's gone."

A young camper is swimming in a river.

A man walks up and asks, "What are you doing in there?"

He says, "I'm washing my clothes."

The man asks, "Why don't you use a washing machine?"

The camper says, "I tried that, but I got too dizzy."

I came across two talking stones
while I was camping.
One was big but shy. The other was a little
boulder.

Why shouldn't you tell a joke
while you are ice fishing?
The ice will crack up.

Game warden: Didn't you see the "No
Fishing" sign?

Boy: I'm not fishing, sir. I'm teaching
these worms how to swim!

Where do fishermen go to
get their hair cut?
The bobber shop.

What did the fisherman say to the magician?
Pick a cod, any cod!

Why did the lonely man go fishing?
To find a gill friend.

What kind of music should you listen to while fishing?

Something catchy.

Sherlock Holmes and Dr. Watson went on a camping trip.

After a good meal, they laid down for the night and went to sleep.

Some hours later, Holmes awoke and nudged his faithful friend. "Watson, look up at the sky and tell me what you see."

Watson replied, "I see millions and millions of stars."

"What does that tell you?"

Watson thought for a minute. "It tells me that there are millions of galaxies, and potentially billions of planets. I can deduce that the time is approximately a quarter past three. I can see that God is all powerful and that we are small and insignificant. I also suspect that we will have a beautiful day tomorrow. What does it tell you?"

Holmes was silent for a minute, then spoke. "It tells me that someone has stolen our tent."

Knock, knock.
Who's there?
Eel.
Eel who?
Eel you go fishing with me?

What did the fishing pole say to the fish?
Catch you later!

How do you communicate with a fish?
You drop it a line.

What do you catch when you go ice fishing?
A cold.

Why didn't Noah do much fishing on the ark?
He only had two worms.

Two men go on a fishing trip.

They rent all the equipment: reels, rods, waders, a rowboat, a car, and even a cabin in the woods. They spend a fortune.

The first day they go fishing, they don't catch anything.

The same thing happens on the second day and the third.

It goes on like this until finally, on the last day of their vacation, one of the men catches a fish.

As they're driving home, they are very disappointed. One man turns to the other and says, "Do you realize that this one lousy fish we caught cost us over a thousand dollars?"

The other man says, "Wow! Then it's a good thing we didn't catch any more!"

**Why is it so easy to weigh a
fish after you catch it?**
It has its own scales.

**Did you hear about the fisherman
who accidentally caught a dolphin?**
He didn't do it on porpoise.

What is the best way to catch a fish?
Have someone throw one at you.

**What do you get when you cross a
fishing lure with a gym sock?**
A hook, line, and stinker.

7

Away from Home on Vacation: At the Pool and Beach

Why did the dolphin cross the beach?
To get to the other tide.

What do frogs like to eat at the beach?
Hopsicles.

**Why didn't the puppy want
to go to the beach?**
He didn't want to be a hot dog.

How do swimmers clean themselves?
They wash up on shore.

**What did Cinderella wear on her
feet when she went for a swim?**
Glass flippers.

What did the pig say on a hot summer day at the beach?
I'm bacon out here.

What do you get when you cross an elephant and a fish?
Swimming trunks.

What kind of rocks do you never find in the ocean?
Dry ones.

Why do people like to go swimming in salt water?
Pepper water makes them sneeze.

What's the best day of the week to go to the beach?
Sunday.

Why wasn't the girl afraid when she swam past a shark in the ocean?
Because it was a man-eating shark.

What is a polar bear's favorite swimming stroke?
The blubber-fly.

**What did the ocean
say to the shore?**
Nothing—it just waved.

**What do you call a cat
who lives at the beach?**
Sandy claws.

**What washes up on
very small beaches?**
Micro-waves.

**Why did the swimmer keep
doing the backstroke?**
She just had lunch and didn't
want to swim on a full stomach.

Did you hear about the kidnapping at the beach?
It's okay—he woke up.

What makes spiders good swimmers?
They have webbed feet.

What exercise is best to get ready to go swimming?
Pool-ups.

What did the family do when they arrived at the beach?
They shellabrated.

What did the beach say when the tide came in?
Long time, no sea.

What do you call seagulls that live by the bay?
Bagels.

What's the best place to sleep at the beach?
The seabed.

What did one tide pool say to the other tide pool? Show me your mussels.

What direction do chickens swim in the pool?
Cluck-wise.

Why is it a bad idea to swim on a full stomach?
Because it's much easier to swim in water.

Someone knocked on my door and asked for a small donation for the local swimming pool.
I gave him a glass of water.

What do fish use as money?
Sand dollars.

**What kind of sandwich can
you make at the beach?**
Peanut butter and jellyfish.

**What swimming stroke do
sheep enjoy the most?**
The baaaackstroke.

**What card game should
you bring to the beach?**
Go Fish.

8

Bonus: Travel, Tourism, and Geography

How can you tell elephants love to travel?
They always pack their own trunk!

A time traveler was in a restaurant.
He liked it so much he went back four seconds.

Why did the robot go on vacation?
To recharge its batteries.

What do you find in the middle of nowhere?
The letter H.

Knock, knock.
Who's there?
Alpaca.
Alpaca who?
Alpaca suitcase, you load up the car.

Why is it impossible to starve in the desert?

Because of all the sand which is there.

What is gray and has four legs, a tail, and a trunk?
A mouse going on vacation.

What do you call a snowman on summer vacation?
A puddle.

What did the volcano say to his son?
"I lava you."

What does bread do on vacation?
It just loafs around.

What is brown, hairy, and wears sunglasses?
A coconut on vacation.

Why are mountains the funniest travel destinations?
Because they're hill areas.

What do you have if you are carrying two suitcases in one hand and three in the other?
Really, really big hands!

What has a mouth but can't eat?
A river.

Why did the pirate go on vacation?
He wanted to get a little ARR and ARR.

What travels around the world but stays in one corner?
A stamp.

Have you heard the joke about the skunk who went on vacation?
Never mind—it really stinks.

While fishing off Myrtle Beach, a tourist capsized his boat.

Petrified, he yelled to an old guy standing on the shore, "Are there any gators around here?!"

"Naw," the man hollered back, "they ain't been around for years!"

Feeling safe, the tourist started swimming toward shore.

Halfway there, he asked the guy, "How'd you get rid of the gators?"

"We didn't do anything," the old guy said. "The sharks got 'em."

Why don't mummies go on vacation?
They're afraid to relax and unwind.

What do islands and the letter T have in common?
They're both in the middle of water.

What is in the middle of the sea?
The letter E.

Did you hear about the tourist who broke his left leg and arm?
He's all right now.

Where do cows go on vacation?
Moo York.

Why do paper maps never win poker tournaments?
Because they always fold.

Why couldn't the astronaut book a hotel room on the moon?
Because it was full.

Why can't basketball players go on summer vacation?
They'd get called for traveling.

Where do math teachers go on vacation?
Times Square.

What kind of footwear do frogs wear on vacation?
Open toad shoes.

Why do birds fly south for the winter?
Because it's too far to walk.

Do fish go on vacation?
No, they're always in school.

Where do pianists go for vacation?
The Florida Keys.

Where can you find an ocean without water?
On a map.

Where is the ocean the deepest?
At the bottom.

Collect All These Great Joke Books!

Lots of Jokes for Kids
ISBN: 9780310750574

Lots of Knock-Knock
Jokes for Kids
ISBN: 9780310750628

Lots of Christmas Jokes
for Kids
ISBN: 9780310767107

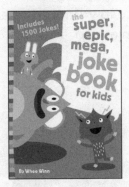

The Super, Epic, Mega
Joke Book for Kids
ISBN: 9780310754794